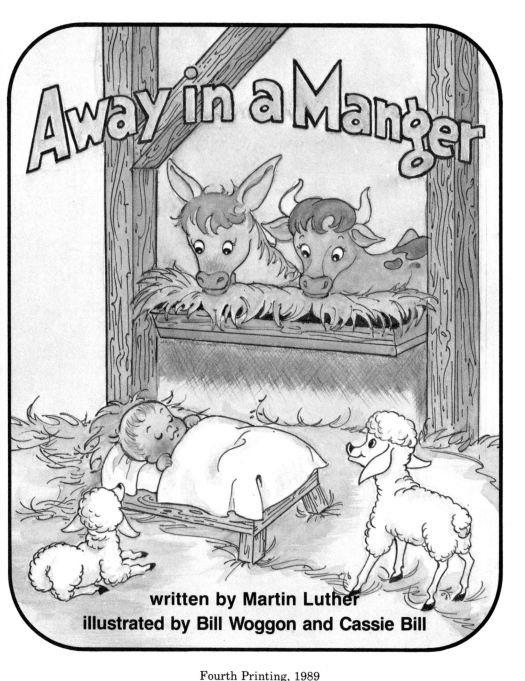

Away in a Manger

written by Martin Luther

illustrated by Bill Woggon and Cassie Bill

Fourth Printing, 1989
Library of Congress Catalog Card No. 84-052167
© 1985. The STANDARD PUBLISHING Company, Cincinnati, Ohio.
Division of STANDEX INTERNATIONAL CORPORATION. Printed in U.S.A.

Away in a manger,

no crib for His bed,

The little Lord Jesus

laid down His sweet head;

The stars in the sky—

looked down where He lay,

The little Lord Jesus,

asleep on the hay.

The cattle are lowing,

the poor baby wakes,

But little Lord Jesus,

no crying He makes.

I love Thee, Lord Jesus,

look down from the sky,

And stay by my cradle

till morning is nigh.

Be near me, Lord Jesus,

I ask Thee to stay

Close by me for ever, and love me I pray.

Bless all the dear children in Thy tender care,

And take us to Heaven to live with Thee there.

Away in A Manger

Martin Luther

Arranged by
Carl Mueller

1. A - way in a man - ger, no crib for His bed, The lit - tle Lord Je - sus laid down His sweet head; The stars in the sky looked down where He lay, The lit - tle Lord Je - sus, a - sleep on the hay.

2. The cat - tle are low - ing, the poor ba - by wakes, But lit - tle Lord Je - sus, no cry - ing He makes. I love Thee, Lord Je - sus, look down from the sky, And stay by my cra - dle till morn - ing is nigh.

3. Be near me, Lord Je - sus, I ask Thee to stay Close by me for ev - er, and love me I pray. Bless all the dear chil - dren in Thy ten - der care, And take us to Heav - en to live with Thee there.